First published in 2012
by Black & White Publishing
29 Ocean Drive, Edinburgh EH6 6JL

1 3 5 7 9 10 8 6 4 2   12 13 14 15

ISBN: 978 1 84502 415 4

Copyright © Cameron McPhail 2012

Designed and typeset by Ellipsis Digital Ltd, Glasgow
Printed and bound by Hussarbooks, Poland www.hussarbooks.pl

Contents

1 April 2012

Dear Candidate

A Message from the Examination Board

With the advent of global warming, Scotland is set to become a paradise with long, hot summers and short, warm winters. An illustrated guide to the new Scotland follows this letter.

However, it is anticipated that this dramatic climate change will lead to an unsustainable influx of people to Scotland. To avoid this and the associated pressure on our land, resources and infrastructure, the Scittish Government have agreed to introduce a formal test for all aspiring Scottish residents. Although the process may be daunting, it is believed that the Scottish Nationality Test is the fairest way of managing a difficult situation.

It is expected that there will be places for a wide range of applicants, but priority will be given to those with the following skills:

- Dentists
- Cosmetic surgeons
- Footballers
- Numerate bankers
- Dieticians
- Glamour models

If you are already resident in Scotland you need not take this test, unless you are living in any of the following more dubious areas of Edinburgh or Glasgow:

- Morningside
- Newton Mearns
- The New Town
- Bearsden

It is anticipated that competition will be fierce for a home in the New Scotland and many will unfortunately be disappointed not to secure a place in our Garden of Eden. The government regrets that we cannot take in more candidates, but the reality of the situation dictates otherwise. In particular and despite the plight of Saxonia (previously known as England) post-global warming, there will be a very strict quota on candidates wishing to move to Scotland from South of the Demilitarised Zone.

We wish you well with the test and I hope that your years of diligent study bear fruit.

Di Aspora

pp
Dr Rab Scallion
Chairman, Examination Board

Post-Global Warming:
An Illustrated Guide

With global warming almost upon us, the next few pages illustrate some of the more profound changes Scotland can expect to see over the next few years. On the left-hand side of each page are photographs of the country as we know it now. And on the right-hand side are images of the same scenes post-global warming.

July in Millport

Brodick Harbour, The Isle of Arran

Outdoor Pursuits, The Scottish Borders

Drumchapel

The World Pipe Band Championships, Dunoon

Highland cattle, Perthshire

Completing the Test

Instructions

- Candidates should at least attempt to read all the questions

- Candidates have a fortnight to complete the test

- To avoid burnout, it is suggested that you only attempt one section at a time

- Please use only tartan ink

- Candidates may confer as they see fit, but it's unlikely to help

- Marks may be dedacted for bad spelling

- Due to budget cuts candidates are responsible for marking their own paper. The answers are provided in Appendix 1

Bonus Opporchancities

Candidates will also be asked to complete a set of more advanced questions. These Bonus Opporchancities are clearly marked throughout the paper. Subject to availability and the payment of a discretionary administration fee, candidates answering one or more of these questions successfully will be granted residency in one of the following Scottish High Status Areas:

- Portree
- Airdrie
- Bathgate
- Barlanark

Street Talk

In several sections candidates are asked to answer a set of 'Street Talk' questions. These are designed to measure applicants' awareness and understanding of contemporary Scottish life. To comply with the privacy laws, the names of actual commentators have been changed, for example:

'Immigrants have always brought something special to Scotland.'

Nan Bread and Chris P. Duck

Frequently Asked Questions

These are covered in Appendix 2 and include guidance on several key issues, for example:

Q: *Will fry-ups still be kosher?*

A: Technically speaking, fry-ups were never really kosher, however current culinary practices will continue but couscous may, on occasion, be substituted for chips

Including all bonus opporchancities there are 300 marks available in the test. Candidates scoring at least 150 or 50% will be deemed to have passed. However, and irrespective of the scores achieved in other sections, a candidate will also be expected to score over 80% in the sections on Gender Studies and Scottish Sports Studies.

The higher the candidate's score, the better the choice of location available to prospective new residents. For example:

Test Score %	Illustrative Location (Post-Global Warming)
51–60	Stornoway
61–70	Byres Road
71–80	Govan
81–100	Sighthill, Edinburgh

50–60% Stornoway

© Shutterstock

61–70% The Byres Road

© Shutterstock

71–80% Govan

© Shutterstock

81–100% Sighthill, Edinburgh

© Shutterstock

The Test Paper

1 Gender Studies

1.1 *Which one of the following statements does not reflect the attitude, behaviour and beliefs of the average Scottish male?*

(i) To control the TV remote is to control the world ☐

(ii) Dirty dishes migrate automatically to the dishwasher ☐

(iii) Toilet rolls grow naturally on their holders ☐

(iv) An empty milk carton goes back into the fridge and not the bin ☐

(2 marks)

1.2 *Given the text below, are you:*

(i) An old soldier ☐   (ii) A lesbian ☐   (iii) Both ☐

The kilted old soldier, complete with a chestful of medals, sat down at Starbucks in George Street, Edinburgh, ordered a cappuccino and started re-reading his treasured copy of *The History of the Highland Light Infantry*. As he slowly sipped his coffee, a young woman sat down next to him.

She turned to the old soldier and asked, 'Were you a real soldier?'

3

He replied, 'Well, I spent my whole life in the HLI
fighting Germans, Japanese and Communists, so yes
I am an old soldier. And you, what are you?'

She said, 'I'm a lesbian. I spend my whole day thinking
about naked women. As soon as I get up in the
morning, I think about naked women. When I shower, I
think about naked women. When I watch TV, I think
about naked women. It seems everything makes me
think of naked women.'

The old soldier looked quizzically at the lady, nodded
and then returned to his book.

A little while later, a young man sat down on the other
side of the soldier, noticed that he was reading *The
History of the Highland Light Infantry* and casually
asked: 'Are you a soldier?'

He replied, 'I always thought I was, but I've just
discovered that I'm a lesbian.'

(2 marks)

1.3 What is not an appropriate term for a beautiful woman with a ginger-bearded Scotsman?

(i)	Blind	☐
(ii)	Desperate	☐
(iii)	Mismatched	☐
(iv)	A hostage	☐

(2 marks)

1.4 From the passage below, was the Perth man's wife:

(i)	A rocket scientist?	☐
(ii)	A brain surgeon?	☐
(iii)	Flaxen-haired?	☐

On a bitterly cold winter morning in Blairgowrie a couple were listening to the radio over their breakfast. It came as no surprise when the announcer said, 'Perthshire is expected to have eight to ten inches of snow today, so please park your car on the even-numbered side of the street to allow the council's snowplough to get through.' Immediately the community-minded wife went out and moved her car.

Exactly a week later the same radio announcer said, 'Perthshire is expecting eight to ten inches of snow today, so please park your car on the odd-numbered side of the street to allow the council's snowplough to get through.' The diligent wife went out and moved her car again.

The next week the couple were again having breakfast, when the radio announcer said, 'We are expecting eight to ten inches of snow today, so ....' Just then the electricity was cut. The wife was very upset, and with a worried look on her face she said, 'Hugh, I don't know what to do. Which side of the street do I need to park on so the council's snowplough can get through?'

Then with the love and understanding gleaned from twenty years or marriage, the husband gently replied:

'This time luv, why don't you just leave the car in the garage.'

(2 marks)

Bonus Opporchancity

1.5 A recent Inversnecky University survey on the attitudes of Scottish women towards Scottish men provided many penetrating insights into the female mind. Which of the following quotes are taken directly from that acclaimed study?

(i)   The average Scottish male thinks that he isn't ☐
(ii) I asked my husband, 'If you can't live without me, then why aren't you dead yet?' ☐
(iii) Scottish men do cry, but only when ironing ☐
(iv) For Scottish men sex is the most beautiful thing that money can buy ☐

(4 marks)

1.6 The Scottish male has an enviable reputation for engaging the ladies in conversation and quick-witted banter. Which of the following quotes represents the Scottish male at his most engaging best?

(i)   Are you going to finish that drink? ☐
(ii) I want you to have my children – they're in the car outside ☐

(2 marks)

1.7 *In the extract below, do you believe that Big Ali's concern is that, 'hell hath no fury like a Scottish woman scorned'?*

(i) Yes ☐   (ii) No ☐

Rob is at work one day when he notices that his mate Big Ali is wearing an earring. Rob knows Ali to be a conservative man and is curious about his sudden change in 'fashion sense' so Rob asks:

'What's wi the jewellery? Bit auld fir that, int yi?'

'It's no big deal, it's only an earring,' Ali replies sheepishly.

Rob lets it lie, but then his curiosity gets the better of him and he asks:

'So, how long huv yi bin wearin one?'

Reluctantly Ali replies, 'Ever since the wife found it in the back seat of the car.'

(2 marks)

1.8 MacSingles online and newspaper dating is Scotland's fastest-growing pastime. From the following selection of recent 'male seeking female' ads, candidates are asked to identify the ones which capture the essence of the Scottish male psyche. Below is a glossary of frequently used terms and acronyms provided for candidates who may be unfamiliar with the language used by MacSingles participants:

MacSingles Dating: Some Frequently Used Terms

DDF	Disease and drug free
DG	Damaged goods
DTM	Desperate to meet
FILP	Fully index-linked pension
MBA	Married but available

(i)   DDF male, forty-five, Glasgow area shelf stacker, seeks twenty to twenty-five-year-old who puts out on the first date and is interested in fortified wine, Sky Sports, eating with her fingers and starting bare knuckle fights in an empty room ☐

(ii) Bitter, disillusioned flame-haired Keppoch
bundle of mischief seeks wealthy lady for
bail purposes. DG so GSOH required.
No retreads please ☐

(iii) Sub-prime MBA Niddrie man, twenty-seven,
medium build, some brown hair, bloodshot
eyes seeks cast iron alibi for the night of
February 27 between 8.00pm and 11.30pm ☐

(iv) Self-made man from Larkhall with own
caravan and FILP DTM equally sophisticated
and solvent lady for long weekends at
Seaton Sands and to share the Calor Gas costs ☐

(4 marks)

TOTAL AVAILABLE IN THIS SECTION: 20 MARKS

CANDIDATE'S SCORE FOR THIS SECTION: _____ MARKS

II Scottish Language

2.1   Although only some forty miles apart, the citizens of Edinburgh and Glasgow often use completely different words to convey the same meaning. Bearing this in mind, candidates are asked to consider whether the two lists below have been compiled correctly.

(i) Yes ☐   (ii) No ☐

Edinburgh Words	Glasgow Words	Edinburgh Words	Glasgow Words
Excitable	Mental	Downcast	Scunnered
Contretemps	Stooshie	Accountant	Pochler
Middleclass	Minted	Altercation	Stramash
Easy	Scoosh	Absent-minded	Hiedtheba
Questionable	Atspish	Lucky	Spawney
Auditor	Clype	Ensuite	Chantie

(2 marks)

2.2 *A humorous contradiction in terms, more properly known as an oxymoron, is one of the many delights of the Scottish language. Which of the following such expressions were shortlisted for the coveted Harsh But Fair award at the recent Edinburgh symposium on the subject?*

(i)   Understanding judge   ☐

(ii)   Sun-drenched Fair Fortnight   ☐

(iii)   Come oan, get aff   ☐

iv)   Head butt   ☐

(v)   Dundee, City of Discovery   ☐

(vi)   Karaoke singer   ☐

(vii)   Scottish BBQ   ☐

(viii) Solvent bank   ☐

(ix)   Paisley University   ☐

(x)   Sunshine in Leith   ☐

(4 marks)

2.3 Regional differences in dialect can cause serious misunderstandings in Scotland. In one sentence please summarise what has actually gone wrong in the court case reported below.

A plummy Advocate Depute from Edinburgh was questioning a Wishaw nyaff during a robbery trial.

Advocate: 'You say you went up to your friend's house that night. Why did you go there?'

Witness: 'Tae get a tap.'

Advocate: 'Is your friend a plumber?'

Witness: 'Naw.'

Advocate: 'Are you a plumber?'

Witness: 'Naw.'

The witness is a bit bewildered by this line of questioning and the Advocate realises it, but he also notices that the court's police officer is helpfully rubbing the fingers of one hand together in the universal gesture of money. Daylight eventually dawns on the Advocate and he changes his line of questioning accordingly.

Advocate: 'So you went to the house to borrow money?'

Witness: 'Naw.'

Advocate:	'Ah. You went to the house to lend money?'
Witness:	'Naw.'
	In exasperation the Advocate says:
Advocate:	'You told the court you went to your friend's house for a tap. What kind of tap was it?'
Witness:	'A Celtic tap.'

Answer _____ **(4 marks)**

2.4 *From the five pairs of weather-related synonyms presented below, candidates are asked to decide which is the cissier of the two nations.*

(i) Saxonian Word ☐   (ii) Scottish Equivalent ☐

Monsoon	Sunny intervals
Hurricane	Squall
Winter	Summer
Flood	Puddle
Golf ball	Hailstone

(4 marks)

Bonus Opporchancity

2.5 Scotland is a patchwork of colourful and evocative dialects. With this in mind, the following tale should be read out loud in Doric, the north-eastern dialect of Scotland. Once candidates have reflected on the passage, they should then decide whether they sympathise with the girl's confusion.

(i) Yes ☐   (ii) No ☐

Two rural Aberdeenshire girls went into Aberdeen to get their passport photos taken. When the very old-fashioned photographer went behind his antique camera and pulled the black cloth hood over his head the following conversation ensued between the two girls:

'Fit's he daein?'

'He's jist gonna focus.'

'Fit, baith at the same time?'

(4 marks)

2.6 *The Scottish language is always evolving and innovating. Please consider which of the following recent additions to the nation's 'wurds' has been incorrectly defined.*

(i) **Cashtration**: What most Scots feel as the end of the month approaches ☐

(ii) **Ignoranus**: A Jobsworth who's both stupid and an ass ☐

(iii) **Foreploy**: Any male Scottish strategy devised solely for the purpose of getting sex ☐

(iv) **Coffee**: Edinburgh word for the person upon whom one coughs ☐

(4 marks)

TOTAL AVAILABLE IN THIS SECTION: 22 MARKS

CANDIDATE'S SCORE FOR THIS SECTION: ⎯⎯ MARKS

III Politics and International Relations

3.1 *Did the incident reported below further weaken the already fragile diplomatic relations between Scotland and Saxonia?*

(i) Yes ☐   (ii) No ☐

A Saxon and a Scotsman were sitting around talking one afternoon over a beer. After a while the Saxon says to the Scotsman:

'If I was to sneak over to your house and sleep with your wife while you were off golfing, and she fell pregnant and had a baby, would that make us related?'

The Scotsman cocked his head sideways, squinted his eyes, and obviously thinking hard about the question, finally says:

'Well, I don't know about being related, but it would make us even.'

(2 marks)

3.2 *Under the Geneva Convention which of the following longstanding Scottish traditions are now considered to be torture?*

(i) Strip the Willow ☐   (iii) Glen Michael's Cavalcade   ☐
(ii) Burns Night   ☐   (iv) World Cup Qualification   ☐

(4 marks)

3.3 *Candidates are asked to decide why the multinational encounter described below is fictional because:*

(i) Mermaids don't exist ☐

(ii) Mermaids can't talk ☐

A Scotsman, Saxon and Irishman were walking along a remote Hebridean beach when they came across a mermaid. They immediately struck up a playful conversation.

The Irishman asked whether the mermaid had ever been kissed. She blushed and said 'no' so the Irishman kissed her and she giggled.

Taking up the challenge the Saxon then asked her if she'd ever been fondled. The mermaid blushed and said 'no' so the Saxon duly obliged and she giggled.

The brave Scotsman then asked if she'd ever been shafted. The mermaid blushed and said 'no'.
The Scotsman said, 'well you have now, the tide's gone out.'

(2 marks)

Street Talk: Iraq and Chilcot

3.4 *Many Scots were uncomfortable with the reasons given by the previous government for going to war with Iraq. Against this backdrop, and with the recent publication of the* Chilcot Report, *candidates are asked to consider the following three Street Talk quotes and tick the boxes, if any, where they agree with the opinion being voiced.*

(i) 'The Blair government was naively drawn
into the war in Iraq by the Americans.'
A. M. Bushed, Angus ☐

(ii) 'We now know that Blair's insistence that
Iraq presented a "clear and present danger"
was palpable nonsense.'
**UK Government, Dee Clared-War, Miss Takenly,
Miss Leading, A.I. Concerned**, Fort William ☐

(iii) 'Even after the *Chilcot Report*, it remains
unclear who changed the government's
report on the threat posed by
Saddam Hussein.'
Doctor Ed Dossier, Kirkcaldy ☐

(4 marks)

3.5 *Many observers believe that malapropisms[1] appear to have been invented specifically for some of the country's more confused MSPs. Which of the following malapropisms are widely considered to be true?*

(i) 'Certain allegations have been made against me and when I catch these alligators . . .' ☐

(ii) 'After the poor Election result, it may not be much of a constipation, but at least I didn't lose my deposit.' ☐

(iii) 'The SNP's policies are beyond my apprehension.' ☐

1. *Malapropism: creating a ridiculous effect by the unintended replacement of a word with one of a similar sound.*

(4 marks)

3.6 *Does the following diplomatic incident illustrate that Scots and Saxons will fight about anything and everything?*

(i) Yes ☐   (ii) No ☐

A London barrister drives through a stop sign in Glasgow and gets pulled over by a policeman. The barrister thinks that he is much smarter than the local police and he decides to prove this to himself and have some fun at the Glasgow constabulary's expense! The following exchange then unfolds.

Glasgow cop: 'Licence and registration, please.'

London barrister: 'What for?'

Glasgow cop: 'Ye didnae come to a complete stap at the stap sign.'

London barrister: 'I slowed down, and no one was coming.'

Glasgow cop: 'Ye still didnae come to a complete stap. Licence and registration, please.'

London barrister: 'What's the difference?'

Glasgow cop: 'The difference is, ye huvtae to come to a complete stap, that's the law. Licence and registration, please!'

London barrister: 'If you can show me the difference between slow down and stop, I'll give you my licence and registration; and you can give me the ticket. If not, you let me go and don't give me the ticket.'

Glasgow cop: 'Sounds fair. Please exit your vehicle, sir.'

The London barrister gets out of his car and the Glasgow cop takes out his baton and starts vigorously beating the man.

Glasgow cop: 'Now, dae ye want me to stap or just tae slow down?'

(4 marks)

Street Talk: The 2010 UK General Election

3.7 *Which of the following post-2010 Election comments do you agree with?*

(i) 'Gordon Brown left Downing Street before yet more economic yoghurt hit the fan.'
Justin Thymne, Moffat ☐

(ii) 'Farewell to Lord Mandelson who was unelected, Machiavellian, financially tainted.'
Andy Fibbed, Balloch ☐

(iii) 'Five minutes into the General Election campaign and I was fast asleep.'
Anne E. S. Thetic, Kippen ☐

(iv) 'The Election campaign was just the same old politicians repeating the same old stuff.'
Maureen Thesamevein, Hawick ☐

(v) 'Politicians are just beta males talking about little of any substance.'
Willie Waving, Broughty Ferrry ☐

(2 marks)

TOTAL AVAILABLE IN THIS SECTION: 22 MARKS

CANDIDATE'S SCORE FOR THIS SECTION: _____ MARKS

IV Scottish Medicine

4.1 Which one of the following is considered by doctors to kill the most Scots?

(i) Road accidents ☐

(ii) Waiting for Spring ☐

(iii) Midges ☐

(iv) Black pudding ☐

(2 marks)

4.2 Sir Alexander Fleming, the discoverer of Penicillin, is best remembered in his homeland for:

(i) Being the father of modern medicine ☐

(ii) Saving thousands of wounded soldiers in World War II ☐

(iii) Curing that awkward and difficult-to-explain rash ☐

(2 marks)

4.3 *From the conversation below, please decide whether Jake's future wife is a virgin.*

(i) Yes ☐   (ii) No ☐

Archie and Jake are sitting in the pub discussing Jake's forthcoming wedding.

'Ach, it's all going magic,' says Jake. 'I've got everything organised already: the flooers, the church, the motors, the reception, the rings, the minister, even ma stag night.' Archie nods approvingly.

'I've even bought a kilt to be married in!' continues Jake.

'A kilt!' exclaims Archie. 'That's a great idea, you'll look really smart in that! And what's the tartan?'

'Och,' says Jake, 'I'd imagine she'll be in white.'

(2 marks)

4.4 Scotland is internationally renowned for its breakthroughs in homeopathic medicine. Which of the following such remedies are proven hangover cures?

(i)   Dog hair   ☐

(ii) Irn-Bru   ☐

(iii) The Full Scottish[1]   ☐

(2 marks)

1. *Similar to the Full Saxon but with larger portions and higher levels of both polyunsaturates and carbohydrates*

4.5 Which one of the photographs below is a magnified image of the infamous Scottish midge.

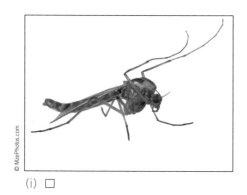

(i) ☐

(ii) ☐

© Mark Gibbons

(iii) ☐

© Getty Images

(iv) ☐

(4 marks)

Street Talk: Scottish

4.6 *As the following selection of e-mails to NHS Direct confirm, Scots suffer from many debilitating medical conditions. Candidates are asked to tick where they have suffered from the conditions mentioned by the correspondents. Note that applicants ticking fewer than three boxes are likely to be considered as having been less than honest.*

(i) 'Dear Doctor, what do the symptoms of a whisky hangover feel like?'
Edna Vice, Bishopston ☐

(ii) 'Dear Doctor, why are Scottish men all so shallow?'
I. Candy, Dunbar ☐

(iii) 'Dear Doctor, I think that there are two sides to the Scottish personality.'
Jacqueline Hyde, Selkirk ☐

(iv) 'Dear Doctor, I have just relocated to a remote Scottish island and I feel alone and all at sea.'
Marie Celeste, St Kilda ☐

(v) 'Dear Doctor, I don't know whether to support Rangers or Celtic.'
Billy Bhoy, Bridgeton ☐

(4 marks)

4.7 *Which of the following is considered to be the most important ever medical breakthrough in Scotland?*

(i)	Clean water	☐
(ii)	Factor 40	☐
(iii)	Filter tips	☐
(iv)	The Fair Fortnight	☐

(2 marks)

TOTAL AVAILABLE IN THIS SECTION: 18 MARKS

CANDIDATE'S SCORE FOR THIS SECTION: ⎯⎯ MARKS

V Sociology

5.1 What is the technically correct term for a small Edinburgh man sandwiched between two irascible Glaswegians?

(i) Short-sighted ☐   (ii) Invisible ☐

(iii) An interpreter ☐   (iv) Other ☐

(2 marks)

5.2 Bingo lives in Drumchapel and Brodie lives in nearby Bearsdenshire. From the information provided below, which is Bingo's paper round?

(i) Paper Round A ☐   (ii) Paper Round B ☐

Newspaper	Copies	Newspaper	Copies
The Herald	23	*Daily Record*	50
Daily Telegraph	10		
The Spectator	8		
Financial Times	6		

(4 marks)

5.3 Would a typical Scot answer true or false to the following statements?

		True	False
(i)	At over £400m, the cost of the Scottish Parliament building represents good value for money	☐	☐
(ii)	Celtic and Rangers would dominate the Saxon Premiership	☐	☐
(iii)	By concocting the name "Senga", Scots illustrated their penchant for making a bad situation much more worser	☐	☐

(4 marks)

5.4 If a party of school children are on a flight from Glasgow to Lourdes, which one of the following schools are they from?

(i)	Hutchesons' Grammar School	☐
(iii)	Fettes College	☐
(ii)	George Watson's College	☐
(iv)	St Margaret Mary's	☐

(4 marks)

5.5 Please read the passage below and decide whether young Murray has a bright future.

(i) Absolutely ☐   (ii) Absolutely not ☐

Teacher: 'Good morning children, today is Thursday, so we're going to have a history quiz. The pupil who gets the answer right can have Friday and Monday off and does not have to come back to school until Tuesday.'

Wee Murray thinks, 'Ya beauty! I'm pure dead brilliant at history so I am. This is gonny be a doddle!'

Teacher: 'Right class, who can tell me who said: "Don't ask what our country can do for you, but what you can do for your country"?'

Wee Murray shoots up his hand, waving furiously in the air.

Teacher, looking round, picks Myles Herrington at the front. 'Yes, Myles?'

Myles (in a refined southern accent): 'Yes Miss, the answer is J. F. Kennedy, Inauguration Speech, 1960.'

Teacher: 'Very good Myles. You may stay off Friday and Monday and we will see you back in class on Tuesday.'

The next Thursday comes around and Wee Murray is more determined than ever to answer the question.

Teacher: 'Who said: "We shall fight on the beaches, we shall fight on the landing grounds . . . We shall never surrender"?'

Wee Murray's hand shoots up, arm stiff as a board, shouting, 'I know. I know. Me Miss, me Miss!'

Teacher, looking round, picks Eloise Smythe, sitting at the front. 'Yes Eloise.'

Eloise (in a very, very posh, Saxon accent): 'Yes Miss, the answer is Winston Churchill, Battle of Britain speech, 1940.'

Teacher: 'Very good Eloise, you may stay off Friday and Monday and come back to class on Tuesday.'

The following Thursday comes around and Wee Murray is hyper, he's been studying *Wikipedia* all week and he's ready for anything that comes. He sits coiled in his wee chair, almost beside himself in anticipation.

Teacher: 'Who said: "One small step for a man, one giant leap for mankind"?'

Wee Murray's arm shoots straight in the air, he's standing on his seat, jumping up and down screaming, 'Me Miss. Me Miss. I know, I know. Me Miss, Me Miss, Meeeeee!!!!!'

Teacher, looking round the class, picks Peregrine Pole-Carew, sitting at the front, 'Yes Peregrine.'

Peregrine (in a frightfully, frightfully, ever so plummy Saxon accent): 'Yes Miss that was Neil Armstrong, 1969, the first moon landing.'

Teacher: 'Very good Peregrine. You may stay off Friday and Monday and come back to class on Tuesday.'

Wee Murray loses the plot altogether, tips his desk and throws his wee chair at the wall. He starts screaming, 'WHERE THE F*CK DID ALL THESE SAXON BAST*RDS COME FROM?'

Teacher spins back round from the blackboard and shouts, 'Who said that?'

Overjoyed, Wee Murray grabs his coat and bag and heads for the door saying, 'Bonnie Prince Charlie, Culloden, 1745. See you on Tuesday Miss.'

(4 marks)

5.6 Candidates are asked to match the following two short stories with two of Scotland's most internationally admired character traits.

    (i) Parsimony ☐   (ii) Compassion ☐

1   A man is delivered to a Glasgow mortuary wearing an expensive, expertly tailored black suit. Big Tam, the mortician, asks the deceased's wife how she would like the body dressed. He points out that the man does look very good in his black suit. The widow, however, says that she always thought her husband looked his best in dark blue. She gives Tam a blank cheque and says, 'I don't care what it costs, but please have my husband in a dark blue suit for the viewing.'

    The woman returns the next day. To her delight she finds her husband dressed in a perfect dark blue suit with a subtle chalk stripe and the suit fits him perfectly. She says to Tam, 'Whatever the cost, I'm very satisfied. You did an excellent job and I'm very grateful. How much did you spend?'

    To her astonishment, Tam returns the blank cheque. 'Nay charge', he says.

    'No, really, I must pay you for the cost of that exquisite suit!' she says.

'Honestly, hen,' Tam says, 'it didnae cost nothin'. You see, a deid gentleman of about your husband's size was brought in shortly after you left yesterday and he was wearing an attractive dark blue suit. I asked his missus if she minded him going to his grave wearing a black suit instead and she said it made nae difference as long as he looked nice. So I just switched their heids.'

2   An elderly Elgin man lies dying in his bed. While suffering the agonies of impending death, he suddenly smells the aroma of his favourite scones wafting up the stairs.

He gathers his remaining strength and gingerly lifts himself from the bed. Leaning against the wall he slowly make his way out of the bedroom. And then, with an even greater effort, he grips the banister with both hands and makes his way tentatively downstairs.

With laboured breath, he props himself against the door frame and gazes into the familiar family kitchen. Were it not for death's agony he would have thought himself already in heaven, for spread out on the kitchen table are dozens and dozens of his favourite scones.

Is this actually heaven? Or is it one final act of affection from his devoted wife of some fifty years, lovingly seeing to it that he leaves this cruel world a happy man?

Mustering one painful final effort he throws himself towards the scones, but can only land on his knees just short of the table. As his aged and trembling hand rises slowly towards the scones his wife suddenly raps his knuckles with her wooden spoon.

'Paws off,' she barks, 'they're all for the funeral.'

(4 marks)

5.7 Which of the following notices were recently spotted outside Scottish churches?

(i) Sunday morning's sermon: 'Jesus walks on water.' Sunday evening's sermon: 'Searching for Jesus.' ☐

(ii) Don't let stress kill you – let the Church help ☐

(iii) For those of you who have children but don't know it, we have a nursery downstairs ☐

(2 marks)

Street Talk: The Credit Crunch's Impact on Scottish Society

5.8 Which of the following two Street Talk comments could apply to many senior Scottish bankers or ex-bankers?

(i) 'Despite losing tens and tens of billions of pounds, not one banker has been charged with any offence.'
Y. Knott, Methil ☐

(ii) 'To conceal their ill-gotten gains, I suspect that many of our disgraced bankers will have set up offshore bank accounts.'
Isla Man, Douglas ☐

(2 marks)

TOTAL AVAILABLE IN THIS SECTION: 26 MARKS

CANDIDATE'S SCORE FOR THIS SECTION: _____ MARKS

6.1 Edinburgh is most aptly described as:

(i) Approximately forty-two miles east of
   Glasgow ☐

(ii) Fine, once they finish building the
   other side of Princes Street ☐

(2 marks)

Street Talk: Global Warming

6.2 Do you agree with the following comment on the impact of Global Warming in Scotland?

(i) Yes ☐   (ii) No ☐

'I am sure that we will really miss the wet and
unpredictable weather.'
Wayne E. Days, Montrose

(2 marks)

6.3 Have the following place names been correctly placed on the map of the UK?

(i) Yes ☐   (ii) No ☐

Place Name	Number
Auchtermuchty	1
Auchinleck	2
Auchterarder	3
Auchenshuggle	4
Aufurfuksake	5

(4 marks)

6.4 Which one of the following icons is often regarded as Scotland's national mascot?

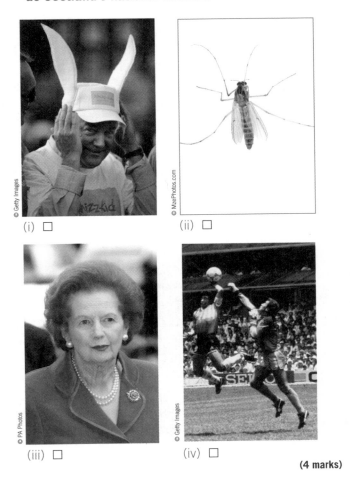

(i) ☐

(ii) ☐

(iii) ☐

(iv) ☐

(4 marks)

6.5 *Having read the passage below, should shark fishing be legal in Scotland?*

(i) Yes ☐   (ii) No ☐

On one of her frequent Scottish tours, the Queen took a day off to visit the Ayrshire coast. Her Majesty's Range Rover was driving along the golden sands of Seamill when she heard a commotion. The Queen rushed to see what was happening and on approaching the scene she noticed that, just beyond the surf, there was a hapless man wearing nothing but a Glasgow Celtic top and frantically struggling to free himself from the jaws of a twenty-foot shark!

At that very moment a speedboat with three men wearing Glasgow Rangers tops sped into view. One of the men took aim at the shark and fired a harpoon into its ribs, immobilising the predator instantly. The other two reached out and pulled the Celtic fan from the water and then, using nothing more than their bare hands, they beat the shark to death.

Having bundled the semi-conscious man and the dead shark into the speedboat, they were preparing to speed off when they saw the Queen beckoning to them from the shore. Not wishing to appear rude, the lads beached their boat and went to see what the Monarch wanted. The Queen went into raptures about the rescue and said, 'I heard that some people in this part of the country were bigoted but I've just witnessed a truly enlightened example of bipartisan harmony which should serve as a model for other Scots.'

Overwhelmed by what she had just seen, she knighted them all on the spot and then drove off feeling proud and uplifted by the selfless example shown by her loyal subjects. As she departed the bemused harpoonist asked the others, 'What was that all about?'

'That,' one answered, 'was our Queen and amazingly she knows everything about our country.'

'Well,' the harpoonist replied, 'she knows nothing about shark fishing. How's our bait holding up? Or should we get a fresh one?'

(4 marks)

6.6 *Global warming is expected to have a profound influence on Scotland's wildlife. From the photographs below and opposite, is the left-hand set of images:*

   (i)   Pre-Global Warming   ☐

   (ii) Post-Global Warming   ☐

(4 marks)

Puffins, St Kilda

The Animal Shelter, Dumfries

Birds of Prey, Torridon

Shetland Ponies, Papa Stour

6.7 For the moment, the Scottish definition of a heat wave is:

(i) A foreign holiday ☐

(ii) The menopause ☐

(iii) A two-bar electric fire ☐

(4 marks)

TOTAL AVAILABLE IN THIS SECTION: 24 MARKS

CANDIDATE'S SCORE FOR THIS SECTION: _____ MARKS

VII Philosophy and Theology

7.1 Candidates are asked to read the following passage and decide whether Fiona's Sunday school children were correct.

(i) Yes ☐   (ii) No ☐

Fiona was testing the children in her local Sunday school class to see if they understood the concept of getting to Heaven.

Fiona asked them, 'If I sold my house and my car, had a big jumble sale and gave all my money to the church, would that get me into Heaven?'

'NO!' the children answered.

'If I cleaned the church every day, mowed the grass and kept everything neat and tidy, would that get me into Heaven?'

Again, the answer was, 'NO!' By now Fiona was starting to smile.

'Well, then, if I was kind to animals and gave sweets to all the children, and loved my husband. Would that get me into Heaven?' she asked them again.

Again, they all answered, 'NO!' and Fiona was just bursting with pride for them.

'Well,' she continued, 'then how can you get into Heaven?'

And the whole class chorused, 'YOU'VE GOT TAE BE F*CKIN' DEID, FIONA!'

(4 marks)

Bonus Opporchancity

7.2 *What is the anthropological significance of the subtle difference in the spelling of the words "Weegi" and "Weegie"?*

GOOGLING STRONGLY ADVISED

Answer _____ **(4 marks)**

7.3 *In Scotland distance is always measured in minutes, so what is time measured in?*

Answer _____ **(4 marks)**

7.4 *Does this parable reflect what most Scots hope life in Heaven is like?*

(i) Yes ☐   (ii) No ☐

A Dundee couple made a pact that whoever died first would come back and inform the other about the sex life after death.

After a long life together, the husband was the first to die and, true to his word, he made contact with his grieving wife:

'Heather . . . Heather.'

'Is that you, Duncan?'

'Yes, I've come back from the other side as we agreed.'

'That's wonderful! What's it like?'

'Well, I get up in the morning and I have sex. I have breakfast and then it's off to the golf course. I have sex again, bathe in the sun and then have sex a couple of more times. Then I have lunch. Another trip around the golf course, then pretty much have sex the rest of the afternoon. After supper, it's back to the golf course again. After that it's more sex until the wee small hours then finally I catch up on some much needed sleep. The next day the same routine starts all over again.'

'Oh, Duncan, you really are in Heaven!'

'Well no, actually I'm a rabbit on the Old Course at St Andrews.'

(6 marks)

7.5 If you were unable to push your grandmother off a bus, then it follows that she must be:

(i) Your father's mother   ☐

(ii) Your mother's mother   ☐

(4 marks)

Bonus Opporchancity

7.6 Why is Lorne sausage called square when it is in fact rectangular?

Answer _____ **(4 marks)**

7.7 *An Edinburgh actuary's philosophy on life can best be encapsulated by which of the following phrases?*

(i) His glass is half full	☐
(ii) His glass is half empty	☐
(iii) Technically, both options are the same	☐

(2 marks)

7.8 *Which one of Scotland's great philosophical thinkers have been attributed with the thought-provoking quotes reproduced below?*

(i) David Hume	☐	(iii) Gordon Strachan	☐
(ii) Thomas Carlyle	☐	(iv) Chic Murray	☐

'It's a small world but I wouldn't want to have to paint it.'

'If something's neither here nor there, then where exactly is it?'

(4 marks)

TOTAL AVAILABLE IN THIS SECTION: 32 MARKS

CANDIDATE'S SCORE FOR THIS SECTION: ＿＿ MARKS

8.1 In 1950 Ian Hamilton and his associates repatriated which of the following national treasures to Scotland from Saxonia in the boot of their car?

(i)   The Stone of Destiny   ☐
(ii) The Elgin Marbles   ☐
(iii) Stonehenge   ☐
(iv) The Wembley goalposts   ☐

(2 marks)

8.2 Do you believe that the grainy black and white photograph reproduced below provides indisputable evidence that the Loch Ness Monster exists?

(i)   Absolutely, never any doubt   ☐
(ii) It's still very difficult to say. It could just be a trick of the light or even a big branch floating on the loch   ☐

(4 marks)

8.3 *From the economically challenged mining villages of the worked out Ayrshire coalfield to the fishing towns of the rugged north-east coast, tartan collar Scotland has developed an irrepressible affection for Country and Western songs. Which of the following such songs topped Scotland's Country Music charts in 1990?*

  (i) 'How Can I Miss You If You Won't Go Away?' ☐

  (ii) 'I Keep Forgettin' I Forgot About You' ☐

  (iii) 'I'm So Miserable Without You It's Like Having You Here' ☐

(4 marks)

8.4 *The last of the great Tartan Army crusades into Saxonia was in 1977. As candidates will already know, after a short battle the Crusaders sacked London, the long-thought-to-be-impregnable capital of Saxonia. Ignoring the deliberate mistake, which of the following two sets of photographs overleaf, Set (i) or Set (ii), was taken during or shortly after the 1977 Crusade?*

Set (i) ☐   Set (ii) ☐   **(6 marks)**

55

Set (i)

© PA Photos

© PA Photos

© PA Photos

© PA Photos

Set (ii)

© Shutterstock

© Shutterstock

© Getty Images

© PA Photos

Bonus Opporchancity

8.5 *Scotland has a rich tradition of producing hauntingly beautiful and melancholic music about some of the more tragic events in the nation's history. Which of the following evocative tunes fits into this category?*

(i)   'The Flowers of the Forest'   ☐
(ii) 'The Skye Boat Song'   ☐
(iii) 'You Take the High Road'   ☐
(iv) 'We're on the March with Ally's Army'   ☐

(4 marks)

8.6 *Understandably, more Scots tell jokes about the bagpipes than actually play the instrument. When did the anecdote reproduced below win the World Bagpipe Joke Telling Contest in Dunoon?*

(i) 1314 ☐   (ii) 1745 ☐   (iii) ☐ 1967

A Saxonman, Irishman and Scotsman are in a bar having a quiet drink when a very confident Octopus walks in and says,

'Hey guys, did you hear that I can play any musical instrument you like?'

Rising to the challenge, the Saxonman gives him a guitar, which the cephalopod plays better than Eric Clapton at his peak.

Upping the ante, the Irishman then gives him a piano that the octopus plays magnificently. Four Chopin 'Préludes' simultaneously.

Finally, and with a hint of a wicked grin, the Scotsman throws him a set of bagpipes and then sits back to watch. The octopus fumbles about furiously for several minutes but fails to produce a single sound from the pipes.

The Scotsman says sarcastically, 'What's wrong, Mr Octopus, can't play the pipes?'

In reply, the increasingly flustered octopus stammers, 'Play it? I'm gonna have sex with the honey as soon as I can get her pyjamas off.'

(2 marks)

8.7 Which of the following three battles do most Scottish historians now consider the result to have been recorded incorrectly at the time?

(i) Flodden: 1513   Scotland 0, Saxonia 1   ☐

(ii) Culloden: 1746   Scotland 0, Saxonia 1   ☐

(iii) Wembley: 1955   Scotland 2, Saxonia 7   ☐

(4 marks)

8.8 Skye TV is rumoured to be close to launching a dedicated Scottish channel and the provisional launch day schedule has just appeared on Wikileaks. Please tick which programmes you can see yourself watching in your new homeland.

SKYE WAN Monday

9.00 am   **News and whair it's pishin doon**   ☐

9.30 am   **How Clatty is Yer Hoose?**   ☐

This week the ladies pay a visit to a man whose wife shot the craw only three days ago and find that the entire hoose is under five inches of dishes and the cludgy is radioactive.

10.00 am The Mags Haney Show ☐

Early mornin' chat show hosted by Stirling's very own former crime clan queen, Mags Haney. As always, the Neds and Sengas settle their petty differences by screaming obscenities and attacking each other with furniture and breadknives, much to the amusement of the viewing public.

12.30 pm News and whair it's pishin doon ☐

1.00 pm Neeburs ☐

Soap opera set in the village of Kinghorn in Fife. This week Archie accuses Auntie Morag of being in league with Lucifer and has her burned at the stake.

2.00 pm Film ☐

Angels Wi' Manky Coupons.

4.00 pm Tam the Tank Engine ☐

Tam goes aff the rails and the Fat Controller is chuffed tae bits.

4.15 pm Boab the Builder ☐

Reality show where Boab is investigated by both Building Standards and the VAT man.

6.00 pm News and whair it's pishin doon ☐

7.00 pm Doaktir Whae ☐

In this week's episode the Scottish time traveller takes the Tardis back tae early summer 1966 and knackers Geoff Hurst's legs wae his sonic Glesca screwdriver.

7.30 pm Torn Faced Cockney Galoots ☐

Eastenders wi' subtitles fir us yins. In tonight's episode, Pauline gets her jotters fae the steamie while the rest o' the cast stoat aboot wi' faces the length o' Leith Walk.

9.00 pm Fitba Players' Burds ☐

Drama surrounding the players of fourth division Inversnecky Strollers and their off-pitch antics. This week Boaby is worried that the club is facing relegation while Moira, his bird, is gettin podgered by the rest of the team and its supporters.

10.00 pm News and whair it's pishin doon ☐

12.30 am The Beechgrove Back-Green ☐

The boys plans tae dae up a gairdin in Niddrie but are scuppered when some local nyaffs borrow the wheelbarra to help transport their cairry-oot from the offie.

2.15 am Close Doon and whair it's still pishin doon ☐

(6 marks)

8.9 A "fiddlers' rally" is now most likely to be held at:

(i)   The Gaelic Mod   ☐
(ii) The Usher Hall   ☐
(iii) The Royal Bank's Headquarters   ☐

(4 marks)

TOTAL AVAILABLE IN THIS SECTION: 36 MARKS

CANDIDATE'S SCORE FOR THIS SECTION: _____ MARKS

IX Business and Banking

9.1 *Over the last twenty years what has been Scotland's most successful export?*

(i) Oil ☐   (ii) Whisky ☐   (iii) Alex Ferguson ☐

(2 marks)

9.2 *Do you believe that the encounter reported below is a true story?*

(i) Yes ☐   (ii) No ☐

On an infamous banker's return to Edinburgh in 2009, he was riding home in his chauffeur driven limousine when he saw two men on the roadside verge eating grass. Disturbed, he ordered his driver to stop and he got out to investigate.

He asked one man, 'Why are you eating grass?'

'After the credit crunch and the collapse of the banks we don't have any money for food,' the poor man replied. 'So we have to eat grass.'

'Well, then, you can come with me to my house and I'll feed you,' the banker said.

'But sir, I have a wife and two children with me. They are over there, under that tree.'

'Bring them along as well,' the banker replied.

Turning to the other poor man he stated, 'You can come along with us as well.'

The second man, in a cowed voice, said, 'But sir, I also have a wife and six children with me!'

'Bring them all as well,' the banker answered sympathetically.

They all bundled into the car, which was no easy task, even in a limo.

Once underway, one of the poor fellows turned to the banker and said, 'Sir, you are too kind. Thank you for taking all of us with you. Now our families will not go hungry.'

The banker smiled thinly and then replied, 'Glad to do the favour. You'll really love my place. I've not been home for a while and the grass is nearly a foot high.'

(4 marks)

Street Talk: The Economic Downturn

9.3 *Which of the following comments do you believe ring true?*

(i) 'There's nothing a small country like Scotland can do about the recession.'
Kaye Serasera, Helensburgh ☐

(ii) 'To kick-start the economy, Scotland must export more.'
Sally Forth, Falkirk ☐

(iii) 'If it is to recover, the Scottish economy should focus more on research and development.'
Pat Pending, St Andrews ☐

(2 marks)

9.4 Between 1992 and 1995 Scotland suffered a significant economic downturn. Who is widely accepted by most Scots to have caused the recession?

   (i)   Margaret Thatcher   ☐

   (iii) Dennis Thatcher   ☐

   (ii) Mark Thatcher   ☐

   (iv) Carol Thatcher   ☐

(4 marks)

9.5 In the eventful decade 2000-2009 which two decisions did The Royal Bank of Scotland's Board get right?

   (i)   Hiring Fred Goodwin   ☐

   (ii) Buying ABN Amro at the peak of the market   ☐

   (iii) Speculating on sub-prime debt   ☐

   (iv) Sponsoring Andy and Jamie Murray   ☐

   (v) Firing Fred Goodwin   ☐

(4 marks)

Street Talk: Fred Goodwin

9.6 *Which of the following Street Talk comments about Fred Goodwin do you agree with?*

(i) 'Fred Goodwin should leave Scotland now.'
Oscar Foxtrot, The Grange ☐

(ii) 'The media should continue to hound Goodwin.'
Tilly Emigrates, Morningside ☐

(iii) 'By 2008 the Shred had no idea how to manage RBS.'
Toulouse Le Plot, Newington ☐

(iv) 'Fred Goodwin was usually more concerned about numbers than people.'
Sue Duko, Bruntsfield ☐

(4 marks)

TOTAL AVAILABLE IN THIS SECTION: 20 MARKS

CANDIDATE'S SCORE FOR THIS SECTION: _____ MARKS

X Applied Mathematics

10.1 In a previous exam which famous Scottish intellectual gave the answer for "find x" shown below?

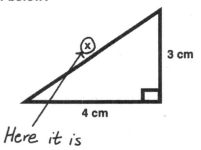

Here it is

(i)   James Clerk Maxwell, Aberdeen University   ☐

(ii) Lord Kelvin, Glasgow University   ☐

(iii) Adam Smith, Glasgow University   ☐

(iv) Frank McAvennie, Celtic and West Ham   ☐

(2 marks)

Bonus Opporchancity

10.2 This is a two-part question.

1. *If a jam sandwich is dropped out of a twenty-storey building 150m high and the initial velocity of said sandwich is zero and G = 9.8/sec² and there is no difference between plain or pan bread, what is the probability of the sandwich reaching the ground?*

   (i)   100% ☐   (ii) 50% ☐

   (iii) 10%   ☐   (iv) 1%   ☐

2. *How many hungry children will testify to your answer?*

   (i)   Fewer than 700   ☐

   (ii) Exactly 700   ☐

   (iii) More than 700   ☐

   (4 marks)

10.3 Muzza and Jaffa stole a 2007 green Toyota 1600GL with a mileage of 35,000 and they were paid £1,000 for the car by Banjo. How much more would they have received from Banjo if the car had been a 2008 registration in metallic silver, had only done 19,000 miles and had four new low-profile tyres?

Answer _____ **(2 marks)**

Bonus Opporchancity

10.4 Banjo Baillie bought half a kilo of cocaine for £20,000. By selling the drugs on his local street corners he hopes to make a 100% profit margin on the transaction. Assuming that Banjo and his two associates, Muzza and Jaffa, consume 10% of the cocaine themselves, and Mad Malky takes his standard 10% cut in protection money, how much must Banjo charge per gram to meet his return on investment target? Candidates may assume cocaine does not attract VAT and, to avoid any adverse consumer reaction, Banjo does not cut his supply with talcum powder.

All workings should be clearly shown

(4 marks)

10.5 *Bianca's personal trainer charges £50 a week, but her trainer can have sex with her whenever he wants. Moira's personal trainer charges £250 a week and has refused to consider sex as payment in kind. Which one of the two women weighs nineteen stone and showers irregularly?*

(i) Moira ☐   (ii) Bianca ☐

(2 marks)

10.6 *Tonto and Monty decided to go to San Francisco to look for "burdz", having been assured by their travel agent that there was a surfeit of single women in the gay capital of California. Late on their second night in the city they were sitting in a bar reviewing their limited progress to date. What does their conversation reported below tell you about Tonto's arithmetic?*

(i) Impeccable ☐   (ii) Suspect ☐

Tonto: 'There's supposed to be eight wimmin for every straight guy in this town.'

Monty: 'Aye, that's what the brochure said.'

Tonto: 'Well, some greedy bastard's got sixteen.'

(2 marks)

10.7 *Edinburgh's Princes Street is some 2,500 yards long. If the economically feasible distance between panhandlers is 100 yards, how many former bankers can make a living on the street? Candidates may assume that they all work on the northern side of Edinburgh's thoroughfare between the hours of 10.00 am and 4.00 pm, with two hours for lunch.*

Answer —————————————————————— **(2 marks)**

10.8 *In the 101st minute of the 1966 World Cup final, a Geoff Hurst shot ricocheted off the West German crossbar, bounced in the goalmouth and away from the danger zone. After some hesitation a goal was awarded by the controversial Russian linesman with the white stick and ultimately Saxonia went on to lift the World Cup. However, using the latest available technology, an Inversnecky University team of experts have reconstructed the events of that fateful day. Their results hinge on a previously overlooked satellite image of the debacle (see opposite). After studying the photograph closely, candidates should answer all three questions posed about the incident (A, B and C).*

Satellite Image of the 1966 Hurst Goal

A *Where does this photograph show that the ball bounced? Candidates may assume that the laws of physics were not suspended and that the camera does not lie.*

   (i) At point ❶ and no goal should have
       been awarded ☐

   (ii) At point ❷ and a goal should have
       been awarded ☐

B *If the ball landed at ❶, then why was the "goal" allowed to stand?*

   (i)   Money changed hands ☐

   (ii) The blind Russian linesman ☐

   (iii) So that Scotland could hammer the
       "World Champions" in 1967 ☐

C *After forty years of mature reflection on the goal,
   does the following statement from a Tartan Army
   spokesman reflect the feelings of Scottish football
   fans?*

(i) Yes ☐   (ii) No ☐

'Nivr in a millyn years pal! Ra Bumble Bee and his
linzman wis baith wrang. The rools clearli state thit the
hail ba his tae be over the hail line, so it diz. And the
satlight ffotaes and slomo all show it wiz nithin likeit. It
wiznae evin close. Bayne and Duckett! It izny right but
weirno bittir. Bygonz is bygonz and we've movd oan wi
oor liffes. The 2010 World Cup in Souffafrika wiz great
wiznit? Germins done the biz ris time, nae mistake.'*

*Please also see page 77, photograph (vi)

(8 marks)

10.9 *Based on the information set out in the exchange
     below, has Tonto's conclusion that 'some greedy
     bastard's got sixteen been confirmed (see
     question 10.6):*

(i)   Yes   ☐
(ii) No   ☐
(iii) You were warned ☐

Just as Monty and Tonto were getting ready to leave the bar in San Francisco, eight single women sashayed into the by now quiet establishment and ordered a round of cocktails. They had obviously been drinking for a while and were clearly intent on having a really good time. Realising that his long wait could soon be over, Tonto immediately went over to strike up a conversation with an attractive brunette. Almost

immediately, however, another one of the group abruptly interrupted Tonto by announcing:

'Don't bother trying to chat any of us up. We're all lesbians.'

Tonto, perplexed but still trying to maintain a cosmopolitan air then asked casually:

'And tell me what part of Lesbiania are yous all from?'

(2 marks)

TOTAL AVAILABLE IN THIS SECTION: 28 MARKS

CANDIDATE'S SCORE FOR THIS SECTION: _____ MARKS

XI Scottish Sports Studies

11.1 *As candidates are no doubt aware, Scotland's lacklustre footballing performance over the last twenty years has left many Scottish males profoundly depressed. Thankfully, the sport of Saxonfreude[1] was developed by Inversnecky University psychologists and the game of Saxon baiting has boosted Scottish self-esteem ever since. Which of the images opposite can be found in Edinburgh's new National Gallery of Saxonfreude?*

1. *Saxonfreude is an old Gaelic word for taking pleasure in the misfortunes of the Saxons. It is thought that the word is in turn derived from the similar sounding German word Schadenfreude*

(i) ☐

(ii) ☐

(iii) ☐

(iv) ☐

(v) ☐

(vi) ☐

11.2 In Saxonia's record (6-3) home defeat by Hungary in 1953, who scored three goals for Hungary in the so-called "match of the century"?

(i) Ferenc Puskás ☐   (iii) Nándor Hidegkuti ☐

(ii) Alan Gilzean ☐   (iv) Dennis Law ☐

(2 marks)

Bonus Opporchancity

11.3 In the space provided below, please tick which of the following classics of Scottish football writing history has a happy ending:

(i) *Partick Thistlenil: The Search for Perfection Continues* ☐

(ii) *Cowdenbeath FC: Positive Thinking's Ultimate Challenge* ☐

(iii) *Brechin City 1906 to 2010: The Wilderness Years* ☐

(4 marks)

11.4 *Following the rise of Andy Murray to the top of tennis in the Greater Dunblane area, several additions to the Scottish Sporting Dictionary have been required. Please tick which of the following words will not be included in the 2012 version.*

(i) *Andyceedents:*   British tennis players before the appearance of Murray   ☐

(ii) *Murrayhome:*   To leave work early and rush home to watch Andy on TV   ☐

(iii) *Andyrexic:*   The teenage Murray   ☐

(iv) *Andynesia:*   The ability to forget all past British tennis failures   ☐

(2 marks)

11.5 *Based on the following tale, should the "two wee boys" go into business some day with Banjo Baillie?*

(i) Absolutely ☐   (ii) Absolutely not ☐

Two supporters are going to an Old Firm match at Parkhead and they find a parking space just outside the stadium.

Two wee boys approach and one wee boy says, 'Gie's a quid mistir and we'll watch yir motur fur yi.'

The man says, 'It's awright son, I'm leavin ma dug in the back seat. He'll watch it.'

The other wee boy says, 'Is the dug any good at pittin' oot fires?'

(2 marks)

11.6 *In a recent newspaper poll which of the following was voted Scotland's favourite international goal of all time?*

(i) Archie Gemmill
(Scotland vs Holland 1974)   ☐

(ii) John Greig
(Scotland vs Italy 1965)   ☐

(iii) MacAdona, Hand of God
(Argentina vs Saxonia 1986)   ☐

(2 marks)

11.7 *As elephants fear mice, so the Tartan Army fears:*

(i) Brazil   ☐   (iii) Argentina   ☐

(ii) West Germany   ☐   (iv) The Faroe Islands   ☐

(2 marks)

11.8 Which Olympic events have the Scots given to the world?

(i) Curling ☐   (iii) Public sector spending ☐

(ii) Hogmanay ☐   (iv) Shark fishing ☐

(2 marks)

11.9 Which of the following are well-known Scottish sporting oxymorons?

(i) Old Firm hegemony ☐

(iv) Alloa Athletic ☐

(ii) SFA Strategy ☐

(v) The Scottish Premier League ☐

(iii) Brechin City ☐

(vi) Hamilton Academicals ☐

(4 marks)

11.10 The final cost for redeveloping London's Wembley Stadium was over £800m, while the cost of rebuilding Glasgow's Hampden Park was a mere £59m. Bearing this in mind, is the football pitch photographed below of:

(i) Wembley Stadium   ☐

(ii) Hampden Park   ☐

© Getty Images

(2 marks)

TOTAL AVAILABLE IN THIS SECTION: 26 MARKS

CANDIDATE'S SCORE FOR THIS SECTION: _____ MARKS

Appendices
So, how Scottish are you then?
Let's find out

I - Gender Studies

1.1   (iv) As the average Scottish male could never be associated with milk.

1.2   (ii) Lesbian. An old soldier would not be drinking a cappuccino, unless perhaps he thought cappuccino was that battle he fought in Italy during the Spring of 1944.

1.3   (ii) Beautiful women are never desperate.

1.4   (iii) Flaxen-haired, as there are no rocket scientists or brain surgeons in Blairgowrie.

1.5   (iii) Scottish men do cry when ironing but only when also asked to take the rubbish out.

1.6   Neither! The correct answer is of course:

'I may not be the best looking guy in here but I am the only one talking to you.'

1.7   (ii) No! Any Scotsman called Big Ali would never be scared of a burd.

1.8   All four are correct and award yourself 2 bonus marks if you added:

'Maryhill intellectual seeks kindred spirit to complete the *Daily Record* crossword.'

The Aberdeen MacSingle in the question would also require certified accounts for the last three financial years from any candidate for the vacancy.

II - The Scottish Language

2.1   (ii) No, as the set of Edinburgh words should all be in Latin.

2.2   All but (viii), as, against all the odds, the Airdrie Savings Bank remains solvent.

2.3   Celtic should have been spelt Sellick.

2.4   (i) Saxonia, but are you really sure that, all things considered, this would not be a better place for you and your family to call home?

2.5   (i) Candidates should indeed be confused, but only because Aberdeen is not, in fact, part of Aberdeenshire.

2.6   (i) In Scotland, Cashtration applies throughout the entire month and not just as payday approaches.

III - Politics and International Relations

3.1   Yes is the correct answer, but candidates could bear
       in mind that, under pending legislation, Scotsmen
       and Saxonians could never really be "related" as the
       story implies.

3.2   All of the answers are correct and 2 bonus marks will
       be awarded to candidates also suggesting New
       Year's Morning or the Scottish Communities League
       Cup.

3.3   Neither option is correct. The encounter was fictional
       but only because Scottish mermaids never blush
       when exposed to sexual innuendo.

3.4   All answers are acceptable. Again candidates may
       award themselves 2 bonus marks if they added:

       'Maybe there are still WMD hidden in Iraq.'

       **Saddam Hussein, May Have-had, Anne Arsenal, U. N.
       Inspectors, May B. Missedit, A. Major Oversight**,
       Peebles

3.5   All answers are correct and this can be stated
       without any fear of contraception. Two bonus marks
       for any candidate adding the classic malapropism:

'Hopefully given the recent election the entire
Scottish Tory Party might fade into Bolivian.'

3.6   (ii) As rogue elements in the Strathclyde Police Force
        mete out this form of treatment to all and sundry.

3.7   Once again all answers are acceptable, but in (i) it
        was not actually yoghurt that hit the fan.

IV - Scottish Medicine

4.1   (ii) Waiting for Spring, although some candidates
        may find waiting for Summer equally depressing.

4.2   None of the answers given is in fact correct. The
        treacherous Fleming is best remembered in Scotland
        for leaving Scotland and going to live in London.
        See Qn 6.3 for the modern Scottish name for
        London.

4.3   (ii) No, as the rascal Archie knows only too well!

4.4   All of the options are correct. Candidates will be
        awarded 2 bonus marks for also adding "cod liver oil
        and the orange juice" to the list although this can
        have unpleasant and often unpredictable side
        effects.

4.5   All options except (iii). This is obviously a Mk1 Dalek
       which looks nothing like a midge and, indeed,
       cannot even fly.

4.6   Of course all are correct. Two bonus marks will be
       awarded for any candidate adding:

       'Dear Doctor, how should Scots tackle their problem
       with alcohol?'

       Percy Veer, Bishopbriggs

4.7   None of the suggested answers is correct. Qn 4.4
       provides the three correct answers.

V - Sociology

5.1   All of the answers are correct and Other should
       include either "toast" or "history".

5.2   (ii) Bingo's paper round and, despite the socio-
       economic distress of many of his customers, he
       makes 50% more in tips than Brodie does in
       Bearsdenshire. Fur coats and no tips?

5.3   True to all three. Nationalism always warps the
       thinking process.

5.4   (iv) St Margaret Mary's. If Hutcheson's, Watson's or
       Fettes were at the airport they would be en route to
       Zurich as part of the school ski trip to Zermatt.

5.5   Absolutely not as an historian: the Battle of Culloden
       was in 1746, not 1745.

5.6   The answers are interchangeable, depending on your
       perspective on life.

5.7   All of the answers are correct. Curiously no one was
       spotted worshipping inside said churches.

5.8   Both answers are acceptable and award yourself 2
       bonus marks if you added the following:

       'Once again investment bankers have only
       succeeded in taking from the rich and giving to the
       poor.'

       Robin Hoods, Banchory

VI - Modern Studies

6.1   Both are correct. However, in the post-credit crunch world candidates could have added either:

The Athens of the North, or

The Reykjavik of the South

6.2   (i) Yes. Given the often perverse and masochistic nature of the Scottish personality.

Two bonus marks if you added the following insightful contribution to the debate:

'Climatic changes are cyclical so global warming may only bring short term benefits to Scotland.'

Elle Nino, Girvan

6.3   (ii) No, only Aufurfuksake is correctly located on the map. Note that Aufurfuksake is twinned with Sodom and Gomorrah.

6.4   None of those illustrated is Scotland's mascot. The correct answer is pictured below.

© PA Photos

6.5   (i) Yes. The real question, however, is whether under the SNP's Republican fringe it will soon be legal to hunt the Queen in Scotland.

6.6   Pre-global warming the answer should be (i), but have you been to the Animal Shelter in Dumfries lately?

6.7   (iii) Technically a one-bar electric fire would suffice if any consumers could afford to switch it on.

VII - Philosophy and Theology

7.1   (i) At the moment the answer is 'yes' but, given the climatic changes facing Scotland, this answer could change!

7.2   'Weegi' is Protestant and 'Weegie' is Catholic, except in mixed marriages where the couple would be known as 'Squeegies'.

7.3   Money.

7.4   (ii) No. All things considered, most Scots do not want to have sex with rabbits and zoologists believe that the feeling is reciprocated.

7.5   (ii) Your mother's mother, but only in Glasgow and environs.

7.6   No one really knows the answer to this particularly perplexing puzzle. Indeed in some butchers Lorne sausage is round.

7.7   All three are wrong: Edinburgh actuaries are trained specifically not to have a "philosophy on life".

7.8   (iv) Chic Murray, who incidentally should never be confused by the equally humorous Andy Murray. Candidates will be awarded 2 bonus marks if they added the Chic Murray quote loved by generations of Scottish immigrants:

'I had a tragic childhood. My parents never understood me. They were Japanese.'

VIII - Scottish History, Culture and the Arts

8.1   All the answers are correct. However, parts of Stonehenge had to go on the luggage rack and the marbles in Hamilton's trouser pockets.

8.2   (i) Absolutely, never any doubt. What further proof would anyone need?

8.3   All three songs topped the country music charts in 1990. Again two bonus marks to any candidates who also added:

'If I Had Shot You When I Wanted To, I'd Be Out By Now.'

8.4   (ii) And candidates should note that Westminster Abbey and the London Eye were indeed transported to Scotland in a subsequent Ian Hamilton expedition.

8.5   (iv) As it recalls the worst ever event in the nation's history, the 1978 World Cup finals in the Argentine.

'Shang-A-Lang' and 'Bye Bye Baby' by the Bay City Rollers are equally lamentable songs and having been written about the same time are now thought to presage the 1978 tragedy.

8.6   (iii) But, as all credible candidates should know, the premise of the question is wrong. This is, in fact, the only joke ever written about bagpipes.

8.7   Sadly none of them. Candidates should also be aware that there was also the rarely spoken about calamity of Wembley 1961: England 9–Scotland 3.

Many Weegis blamed the Weegie goalkeeper, Frank Haffey, for the team's questionable performance on that dark day. There were also counter rumours in Weegie circles that Haffey was more of a Weegi than a Weegie. These have never been substantiated, although the goalie may have once been in a Squeegie relationship.

Haffey's performance also "inspired" the contrived and deeply unamusing Saxonian joke of the time:

'What's the time?'

'Nearly ten past Haffey'.

Unsurprisingly, Haffey emigrated to Australia.

8.8   All but *News and whair it's pishin doon* are
        acceptable answers. Post-global warming this will
        change to *News and whair it's scorchin'*.

8.9   Other than the Airdrie Savings Bank, all bank
        headquarters have now quietly relocated to London,
        so fiddling would surely be out of the question in
        Aufurfuksake.

IX - Business and Banking

9.1   (iii) Alex Ferguson. But up until 2008, The Year of
        the Shred, the answer could have been banking.

9.2   (ii) Absolutely not, it is merely a metaphor for our
        oppressive capitalistic system and any similarities
        with persons either alive or dead is merely
        coincidental.

9.3   All three answers ring true and 2 bonus marks if
        candidates also wrote:

        'When times are tough the government should do
        more to protect Scotland's valuable fishing grounds.'

        Fraser Burgh, Arbroath

9.4　　All four answers are correct. Along with the Baroness Thatcher's father Albert, mother Beatrice, sister Muriel and the two grandchildren, Michael and Amanda.

9.5　　Sadly only one (iv) was correct: sponsoring the brothers Murray. Candidates may have thought that firing Fred Goodwin was a sound, if tardy, decision but actually the Shred 'excused himself' from the top table.

9.6　　Candidates should agree with all comments and avail themselves of 2 bonus marks if they also wrote:

'Most people were delighted when Goodwin left the Royal Bank.'

Gladys Allover, Merchiston

X - Applied Mathematics

10.1　　Unfortunately the question should have read:

Which Scot wrote, 'X marks the spot'? And the answer would have been, 'Robert Louis Stevenson'.

10.2.1　According to the song, it's 1% but it largely depends on how many Weegi seagulls were patrolling the area at the time.

10.2.2 (i) Children living in multi-storey flats will only ever testify that, 'a big boy did it and ran away'.

10.3   £320 or £450 if the getaway driver is included.

10.4   £97.78 per gram, call it £100 to cover shrinkage.

However, as Banjo and his mates are likely to consume 70% of the cocaine and Mad Malky's cut is more likely to be 20%, the likely cost per gram is £320: this higher price also explains the answer to Qn 10.3. Candidates should award themselves 2 bonus marks if they spotted this subtle connection.

10.5   (ii) Logic suggests Moira, but why would a Scot pay a personal trainer £250 a week and still weigh 19st unless of course . . .

10.6   (i) Impeccable. Monty and Tonto were only after straight women.

10.7   Given the fees at Edinburgh private schools, no more than one.

10.8 A (i) is the only acceptable answer. If you have answered (ii), then please hand back your paper to a test supervisor immediately.

10.8 B (i) and (iii). Regarding (ii), although blind, the linesman was in fact Azerbaijani and not Russian. Ironically Azerbaijan's national stadium is named after the linesman, although logic suggests that it would have been more appropriate for the English FA to have changed Wembley's name in his honour.

10.8 C (ii) Cauzz where weeze cum frae, bygonz is nevir bygonz. Thair crewsadz so theyurr.

10.9 (ii) and (iii) and particularly (iii). See the answer to Qn 10.6 for further information.

XI - Scottish Sports

11.1 All images except (ii) and (iv). These pictures are both to be found hanging in the award-winning Glasgow Gallery of Saxonfreude.

11.2 (ii) Nándor Hidegkuti. For Nándor's third goal please see the photograph below.

11.3   Sadly no book about Scottish football ever has a happy ending.

11.4   (iv) Andynesia, as this is how Glaswegians pronounce the name of the South East Asian country largely comprising Java and Sumatra.

11.5   (ii) Sadly these two are more likely to end up firebombing Bingo's lock-up as part of a hostile takeover.

11.6   The correct answer is in fact MacAdona, Hand of God, (Argentina vs Saxonia 1986)

© Getty Images

11.7   Again none is correct. The correct answer is Baroness Thatcher.

11.8   (i) However, Hogmanay was included in a previous Olympics as a demonstration sport but was soon considered to be too dangerous for both participants and spectators.

11.9   All bar (i) are correct. To be oxymoronic "Old Firm hegemony" should have read "Old Firm harmony".

11.10 (ii) Hampden. And at the time of going to print the Wembley surface had been relaid eleven times since 2007 and it is planned to relay the grass up to sixty-five times by 2023. Global warming is likely to make the situation much more worser.

THE SCOTTISH NATIONALITY TEST
FINAL SCORES

SECTION	TOTAL MARKS AVAILABLE	CANDIDATE'S SCORE
1	20	
2	22	
3	22	
4	18	
5	26	
6	24	
7	32	
8	36	
9	20	
10	28	
11	26	
Bonus marks	26	
TOTAL	300	

DO YOU QUALIFY FOR CITIZENSHIP AS A HOT SCOT?

THE RESULTS

0—99 MARKS:

Deep Frozen – that wiz mince. Try again after the next Ice Age.

100—136 MARKS:

Luke Warm – no sae bad. Try, try and try the examiner's patience again sometime.

137—199 MARKS:

Hot Scot – congratulations, you've ~~pissed~~ passed the test! Welcome to the land of milk and honey nut cornflakes, which you need to eat before you can have your square sausage, bacon, eggs, beans and black pudding (chips optional, terms and conditions apply, see small print for details).

200+ MARKS:

Scalding Hot – well done smartypants. Better watch yersel because if you get any cleverer you might spontaneously combust.

Frequently Asked Questions About the Test

Q: *Do we really have to answer all these questions?*

A: It's a little late to be worrying about that now, but no, this is a spoof exam compiled for fun: tackle the test as you wish unless you believe that this answer is a bluff.

Q: *Will Saxon baiting still be legal?*

A: Yes and several of our major universities will offer both undergraduate and postgraduate degrees in the subject. See also Saxonfreude.

Q: *If you had left Scotland, but now wished to return, would that be permitted?*

A: Only under special circumstances and only in Scotland's relatively remote Correction Centres, such as Glenrothes. Such "Previous Scots" may also be required to pay higher taxes and will be unable to work in any of Scotland's Reserved Occupations.

Q: *Will there still be midges in Scotland?*

A: No. Thankfully, midges will be a thing of the past. However, there may be the occasional problem with funnel-web spiders, scorpions and other such troublesome insects.

Q: *Will Glaswegians lose their distinctive accent?*

A: Experts say that over time the Weegie accent is
    expected to become Mediterranean in delivery but
    Glaswegians will still retain that distinctive growl,
    particularly if they have been drinking too many
    margaritas.

Q: *Will a Mediterranean diet be forced on Scots?*

A: Absolutely not! This is just a rumour put about by
    mischief makers bent on stirring unrest in the Tribal
    Heartlands and Tartan Townships.

Q: *Will fry-ups still be kosher?*

A: Technically speaking, fry-ups were never really kosher,
    however current culinary practices will continue but
    couscous may, on occasions, be substituted for chips.

Q: *Could flame-haired Scots be threatened with extinction?*

A: Not necessarily, as it is the government's intention to
    keep citizens with a fair complexion and ginger hair
    indoors during the nine months of summer.

Praise for the Scottish Immigration Initiative

'They better arrive soon before everyone's left.'
Di Aspora

'Immigrants have always been welcome in Scotland.'
P. N. Occhio

'The government should have invited in many more high calibre immigrants years ago.'
Miss D. Boat & Miss D. Opportunity

CONTACT DETAILS

The Exam Board would be delighted to receive material for use in future Scottish Nationality Tests. Please send your contributions in strictest confidence to scotnattest@gmail.com or contact us on Facebook 'Scottish Nationality Test'.